FIVE CHILDREN AND IT

'It' is a Psammead, a sand-fairy, which the children find one day when they are digging in a gravel-pit. It is thousands of years old, and Psammeads, of course, can give wishes – one wish a day, and the wish ends when the sun goes down. Anthea, Cyril, Robert, and Jane think this is wonderful. Their baby brother, too young to enjoy wishes, mostly stays at home, but the others plan to wish for some exciting things.

But what? To be beautiful, to be rich, to fly like a bird? Sometimes it is difficult to think of really good wishes, and very easy to say, 'Oh, I wish . . .' – and then get something that you don't really want. And the Psammead can be very unhelpful. 'Why don't you think before you wish?' it says crossly, when things go wrong.

And things often do go wrong . . .

OXFORD BOOKWORMS LIBRARY

Fantasy & Horror

Five Children and It

Stage 2 (700 headwords)

Series Editor: Jennifer Bassett
Founder Editor: Tricia Hedge
Activities Editors: Jennifer Bassett and Alison Baxter

EDITH NESBIT

Five Children and It

Retold by
Diane Mowat

OXFORD UNIVERSITY PRESS

OXFORD
UNIVERSITY PRESS

Great Clarendon Street, Oxford OX2 6DP

Oxford University Press is a department of the University of Oxford
It furthers the University's objective of excellence in research, scholarship,
and education by publishing worldwide in

Oxford New York

Auckland Bangkok Buenos Aires Cape Town Chennai
Dar es Salaam Delhi Hong Kong Istanbul Karachi Kolkata
Kuala Lumpur Madrid Melbourne Mexico City Mumbai Nairobi
São Paulo Shanghai Taipei Tokyo Toronto

Oxford and Oxford English are registered trade marks of
Oxford University Press in the UK and in certain other countries

ISBN 0 19 422973 4

Illustrated by Claire Pound

Typeset by Wyvern Typesetting Ltd, Bristol
Printed in Spain by Unigraf s.l.

CONTENTS

Chapter 1
Beautiful children

The house was about four kilometres from the station, but after only a minute or two the children began to ask, 'Are we nearly there?' And every time they saw a house they said, 'Oh, is this it?' But it never was. Then they came to the top of a hill, and there was a white house with a green garden and lots of fruit trees. 'Here we are!' Mother said.

Everyone hurried to get out of the carriage – Robert, Anthea, Jane, Cyril, and Martha, the nursemaid, with

Everyone hurried to get out of the carriage.

1

the baby. But Mother did not hurry. The children ran round the house and all through the garden to see what there was. But Mother stood and watched the driver while he carried the boxes into the house.

The children loved the house. They knew immediately that they were going to be happy there. Mother did not like the house very much because it was old and there were no cupboards. But it was deep in the country and after two years in London the children thought that it was wonderful. If you live in London and your family is not rich, you get bored because you cannot go to shops and theatres, and people say, 'Don't do this' and 'Don't go there'. In the country you can go anywhere and do anything.

The White House was on the hill, with a wood behind it and a gravel-pit on one side. It was at the gravel-pit, a week later, that the children found a fairy. Well, that was what it called itself. But it was different from other fairies.

It happened when Mother had to go and stay with Grandmother, who was ill. Martha stayed with the children, of course. But the house was very quiet and empty. The children did not know what to do. Then Cyril said, 'Let's go to the gravel-pit.'

The gravel-pit was very large, with grass and wild flowers round the sides at the top. When they got there, the children decided that they would go down into the pit to play in the sand.

'Let's dig a deep hole – perhaps we can get all the way down to Australia,' said Robert.

The others agreed and they all began to dig hard in the sand. But it was a very hot day. Baby went to sleep and

The gravel-pit was very large, with grass and flowers at the top.

3

Robert, Cyril, and Jane sat down to rest, but Anthea went on working on the hole.

Suddenly she screamed. 'Cyril! Come here! Quick! There's something alive!' she cried.

They all jumped up and hurried over to see what it was.

'It's got feet,' Anthea said. 'And fur. Don't hurt it. I know this sounds stupid, but it said something.'

'What did it say?' asked Cyril.

'It said, "You leave me alone".'

The others just laughed, but the two boys began to move away more of the sand. Soon they could see that there really was something moving in the hole.

Suddenly a hard little voice cried, 'Leave me alone!'

They all jumped back and no one spoke for a minute. Then Robert said, 'But we want to see you.'

'Yes, I wish you'd come out,' Anthea said.

'Oh, well, if that's your wish,' the voice said, and the sand began to fly about everywhere. Then something brown and furry and fat fell out into the hole. 'I think I was asleep,' it said.

The children stood and looked at it. It really was very strange. It could move its eyes in and out on stalks, it had big ears and its body was fat and round and furry. Its legs and arms had soft fur all over them too, and it had hands and feet.

*It really was very strange. It could move
its eyes in and out on stalks.*

'What is it?' asked Jane. 'Shall we take it home?'

The thing turned its long eyes to look at her. 'Does she always say stupid things?' it said.

'She doesn't mean it,' Anthea said. 'Don't be afraid. We won't hurt you.'

The little thing was angry. 'Hurt *me*!' it cried. 'I'm not afraid of *you*!'

'Oh, don't be angry,' said Anthea kindly. 'Tell us who you are. We really don't know.'

'You don't know?' it said. 'Don't you know a Psammead when you see one?'

'A Sammyadd? What's that?' Jane said.

'A sand-fairy, of course. Don't you know a sand-fairy when you see one?'

'I'm not afraid of you!'

It looked very unhappy, and Jane said, 'Of course! I can see that you're a sand-fairy now.'

And Robert said, 'Well, I didn't know that you were a Psammead, but I can see that you are something very wonderful. Please talk some more to us.'

The Psammead looked a little happier when it heard that, and it said, 'Well, you can talk to me, if you want to. Perhaps I'll answer you and perhaps I won't. Now say something.'

At first the children could not think of anything to say, but then Robert asked, 'How long have you lived here?'

'Oh, thousands of years,' the Psammead answered.

The children waited, but the Psammead was silent.

'Please tell us more,' Robert said.

'Well, all right, then,' the Psammead said. 'There were lots of us then,' it went on. 'People sent their children out to look for Psammeads, and when they found us, we gave them a wish.'

'What happened to all the Psammeads, then?' Robert asked.

'Well, if they get wet, they get ill and they usually die, and that's what happened. Most of them got wet and died. And I'm not going to tell you another thing.'

'Oh, just one more question, please,' said Robert. 'Do you give wishes now?'

'You've had one,' said the Psammead. 'You wished to see me, and here I am.'

'Oh, please. Just one more,' Anthea cried.

'Well, all right, but be quick! I'm tired of you!'

It is very difficult to think of a really good wish, in just a second or two. Then Anthea remembered a wish of hers and Jane's. She knew that the boys wouldn't like it, but it was better than nothing.

'I wish we were all very, very beautiful,' she said.

The Psammead pushed out its long eyes and got bigger and fatter, and the children waited. Then it said, 'I'm sorry. I haven't done this for a long time. I'll try again, but I can only do one wish a day for you. Do you agree to that?'

'Yes, oh yes!' the children cried.

'But remember, the wish is only for a day,' said the Psammead. 'When the sun goes down, everything goes back to what it was.'

The Psammead slowly got bigger, then suddenly went small again. 'That's all right!' it said. At once it turned and went back into the sand at the bottom of the hole.

The children stood there for a second, and then Anthea turned to speak to the others. But they were not there! She was looking at three strangers – a girl with beautiful red hair and big blue eyes, and two very good-looking boys. Suddenly she understood. They had their wish. The strangers were Robert and Cyril and Jane – but now they were beautiful. Cyril's hair was golden now, and Robert's was black.

'I liked you better before!' Robert cried angrily to his brother and sisters. 'Jane's hair looks like carrots, and Cyril looks really stupid with long golden hair.'

They went to find Baby, but he was just the same as he was before.

'Perhaps it's because he's young. He can't have wishes. We'll have to remember that next time,' Anthea said, and she held out her arms to him. But Baby's mouth turned down at the corners and then he began to cry loudly. *He did not know them!*

Baby began to cry loudly.

9

It took an hour to stop him crying and then, very tired and cross, they took him home. Martha, Baby's nursemaid, was waiting at the front door. She took Baby from them quickly.

'Where are the others?' she asked. 'And who are you?'

'We're *us*, of course,' Robert said. 'You don't know us because we're beautiful.'

'And we're very hungry,' said Cyril, 'and we want our lunch, please.'

'Go away!' Martha screamed. 'Or I'll send for the police,' and she closed the door in their faces.

The children were very hungry by then, and they tried three times to get into the house – but Martha would not let them in. After a while they went and sat at the bottom of the garden to wait for the sun to go down. 'The wish will finish then, won't it?' Jane said.

But the others didn't answer because no one was really sure.

It was a terrible afternoon. They had no lunch, no tea, and they were tired, angry and afraid. It's true that they were all very beautiful, but that's not a lot of help when you're unhappy. In the end they fell asleep.

It was nearly dark when they woke up. Anthea was the first to wake up and she looked at the others. They were no longer very beautiful. Everything was all right again. Happily, they all went back to the house. Of course,

10

'Go away! Or I'll send for the police.'

Martha was angry. 'Where have you been all day?' she cried.

It is not easy to explain a Psammead to an angry nursemaid, so the children didn't try.

'We met some beautiful children and we couldn't get away from them until it was nearly dark,' Anthea said. 'They were terrible, and we never want to see them again.'

And they never have.

Chapter 2
The children wish to be rich

The next morning Martha took Baby out with her and the children decided to go back to the gravel-pit to look for the Psammead again. At first they could not find it. 'Perhaps it wasn't really here,' Robert said. But they began to dig into the sand with their hands and suddenly they came to the brown furry body of the Psammead. It sat up and shook the sand out of its fur.

'How are you today?' Anthea asked.

'Well, I didn't sleep very well, but thank you for asking,' the Psammead answered.

'Can you give wishes today?' Robert said. 'Because we'd like to have two, if we can. But one is a very little wish.'

'Well, all right,' said the Psammead, looking at Robert with its long eyes. 'Let's have the little wish first.'

'Martha mustn't know about the wishes,' Robert said. 'I mean, she mustn't see anything different about us. And can you do that for every wish on every day?'

The Psammead went a little bigger and then went small again. 'I've done that,' it said. 'It was easy. What's the next wish?'

'We wish,' said Robert slowly, 'to be very rich.'

'How much money do you want?' asked the Psammead. 'It won't do you much good, of course,' it said quietly to itself. 'Well, how much – and do you want it in gold or notes?'

'Gold, please,' Robert said. 'Millions!'

'A full gravel-pit, all right?' said the Psammead, sounding bored. 'But get out before I begin, or you'll die underneath it.'

Its thin arms got very long and it began to move them about. The children were afraid, and ran as fast as they could up to the road. When they were there, they turned to look back. They had to close their eyes and open them again very slowly. The gravel-pit was full, right up to the top, with new, shining, gold coins!

The gravel-pit was full – with new, shining, gold coins.

13

The children stood with their mouths open, and no one said a word.

Then Robert took one of the coins in his hand and looked at it. 'It's different from English money,' he said.

'Well, it doesn't matter. It's gold,' said Cyril. 'Don't forget that it will all go when the sun goes down. Come on! Let's put as much as we can in our pockets and go and spend it.'

So they all put gold coins in their pockets and went off to the village. But the gold was heavy, and soon they were very tired and hot. They decided to get something to drink in the village and then go on to the town of Rochester.

Cyril went into the shop and the others waited outside. But when Cyril came back with a bottle of lemonade, he said, 'I had to pay with *my* real money. When they saw all the coins, they wouldn't change the gold.'

'Well, *I'll* try to get something with the gold,' Anthea said. 'We need a horse and cart. Come on.'

Anthea went to talk to a man who had a horse and cart, and the others waited. After a few minutes she came back, looking very pleased with herself. 'I wasn't stupid like Cyril,' she said. 'I only took out one coin, not all of them, and the man said he'll drive us to Rochester and wait for us.'

On the way to Rochester, they did not speak. They

Anthea went to talk to a man who had a horse and cart.

were making plans about how to spend their gold, and they did not want to talk in front of the driver.

But when they arrived in Rochester, with about twelve hundred gold coins in their pockets, they found that it was very difficult to spend them. Anthea tried to buy a very nice hat, but the woman in the shop looked very strangely, first at the gold coins, then at Anthea.

15

'I can't take that,' she said. 'It's not modern English money.'

They went from shop to shop, but no one wanted to take their gold. 'It's because our hands are dirty and we look untidy. People think we've stolen the gold,' Anthea said.

And it was worse when they tried to buy a horse and carriage. Cyril showed the man his gold, and the man called to his son, 'Send for the police!'

'I can't take that. It's not modern English money.'

16

'It's our money,' said Cyril angrily. 'We're not thieves.'

'Where did you get it from then?' said the man.

'A sand-fairy gave it to us,' said Jane. 'He gives us a wish a day and they all come true.'

The man shook his head slowly. 'Oh dear, oh dear,' he said. 'Stealing, and then telling stories about it.'

Just then a policeman arrived and when he heard about the gold, he said to the four children, 'Come with me. I'm taking you to the police station!'

The children were angry and unhappy, but the policeman walked along the road behind them and they couldn't escape. They held their heads down because they did not want anyone to see them, and suddenly Robert ran into someone. 'Robert, what have you done now?' a voice cried. It was Martha and Baby!

The policeman explained everything to Martha, and Cyril had to take the gold out of his pocket and show it to her.

'I can't see anything – just two very dirty hands,' she said. 'There's no gold there. What are you talking about?'

And then the children remembered that Martha couldn't see the wishes.

It was getting dark when they arrived at the police station. The policeman explained about the gold and the Inspector said, 'Well, let's see it.'

Cyril put his hands into his pockets – but they were empty! The others put their hands into their pockets. They were empty, too! Of course, all the fairy gold went when the sun went down!

'How did they do that?' cried the policeman.

Martha was very angry with him. 'I told you that there wasn't any gold,' she shouted. 'You'll be in trouble for this. Saying that these poor little children are thieves!'

But she was very angry with the children too. 'What were you doing in town alone?' she said to them outside the police station.

And she took them home and sent them to bed early.

Cyril put his hands into his pockets – but they were empty!

Chapter 3
Wings

The next day was very wet. It rained all day and the children could not go to see the Psammead. They stayed at home and wrote letters to their mother. But none of them told her about the Psammead. And the day after that, their Uncle Richard came and took them out, so they did not see the Psammead for two days. But Anthea spent a lot of time thinking about what to wish for.

The next morning, while Martha was busy with Baby, the children left the house quietly and went to see the Psammead. On the way, Anthea said to the others, 'I know what we can ask for – wings!'

The others were silent for a minute, but then they all agreed that they too would like to have wings.

They found the Psammead easily. 'I wish we all had beautiful wings to fly with,' Anthea said.

The Psammead made itself very big and then went small again. The children felt strange for a minute and when they looked, they saw that they had beautiful soft wings of many colours. They moved them about and jumped up and down, and soon they could see the green fields and sunny woods below them and the blue sky

They could fly!

above. They could fly! It was wonderful, and they flew over the woods and trees, the towns and villages, for a long time. But they began to get hungry.

Just then they saw below them some trees full of large red plums. 'We mustn't steal,' Cyril said.

'We've got wings,' Jane answered quickly, 'so we're birds. It's all right for *birds* to take things. Birds can't steal.'

So they flew down onto the trees, and they ate as many of the plums as they could.

They were finishing the plums when they saw a very angry little fat man, who was hurrying through the trees. They were *his* plums and the poor man thought that boys from the village were stealing them. But when he saw that the children had wings, his mouth fell open and his face went green. Anthea did not want to steal anything, of course, so she flew down and pushed some money into his pocket.

'Don't be afraid,' she said. 'We've had some of your plums. We thought that it wasn't stealing, but now I'm not so sure. So that was some money to pay for them.'

The little man sat there on the ground and looked up into the sky. 'Talking birds! Children with wings! This is a lesson for me. From now on, I'm going to live a better life,' he said. And he went into the house and was very kind to his wife.

Plums are very nice, of course, but you soon feel hungry again. So the children stopped first at one house, then another, to ask for something to eat. They didn't get anything because everyone was afraid of them and screamed and ran away when they saw them. By four o'clock they were getting very tired and hungry, so they flew down onto the roof of a church, to think what to do.

'We can't possibly fly all the way home without something to eat,' said Robert.

In the end they decided to take some food from the vicar's house next to the church.

'He's a good man. He'll understand. We'll leave some money for the food,' Cyril said, 'and a note saying that we're sorry.'

Cyril got in through the window and gave the food to the others, who were outside. There was some cold meat, half a cold chicken, some bread and a bottle of soda water. Then they all flew back up onto the church roof to eat it. They were very hungry, so they really enjoyed it. But when you are very hungry, and then you

22

Everyone screamed and ran away when they saw them.

eat a big meal and sit in the hot sun on a roof, it is very easy to fall asleep. And so they did – while the sun slowly went down in the west.

They slept for a long time. When they woke up it was dark – and, of course, they had no wings.

'We must get home,' Cyril said. 'There's a door over there. That's the way down.'

But when they tried the door, they found that it was locked from the other side. They were on top of the church and they had no wings! How were they going to get down?

Anthea put her arm round Jane, who was beginning to cry. 'It will only be for one night,' she said.

Then Cyril said, 'I know. Let's shout! The lights are on in the vicar's house. Someone will hear us and get us down.'

So they shouted and screamed as loudly as they could, and the people in the house heard them. The vicar ran out with his servant.

'Someone is murdering somebody in the church!' the vicar said, afraid. 'Perhaps it's the thief who stole the cold chicken and things.'

But they could not understand why the voices were coming from the sky. So the children shouted, 'We're up here – on top of the church!'

The two men were still afraid, but, slowly and carefully,

The vicar ran out with his servant.

they went up the stairs inside the church. When they came to the top, the vicar shouted through the closed door, 'How many of you are there? Have you got guns?'

'There are four of us, and, no, we haven't got guns,' Cyril answered.

Slowly, the vicar opened the door.

'Good Heavens!' he cried. 'They're children!'

'Oh, please take us down,' cried Jane.

So the vicar and his servant took them down and into the vicar's house. Of course, the vicar wanted to know why the children were on the church roof.

'We went up there because we wanted to see what it was like,' said Cyril. 'But then we couldn't get down again because the door was locked.' He didn't say anything about the wings, of course.

'But who locked the door?' the vicar asked.

'We don't know,' Jane answered. 'But we're not telling you everything.'

'Ah! There's a friend in it, then,' said the vicar's servant man, who was called Beale.

'Yes, but we can't tell you about him,' said Anthea, thinking of the Psammead. 'We really are *very* sorry, and please can we go home now?'

The vicar still did not understand, but he was a kind man, so he sent the children home in a carriage with his servant. Martha, of course, was very angry with them, but Mr Beale explained everything very well. He was a good-looking young man with a nice smile, and after a while Martha forgot to be angry.

So the day ended happily after all.

Chapter 4
Bigger than the baker's boy

The next morning Martha said that the children could not go out. 'You can stay in and be good,' she said.

'There's something that we all want,' said Robert. 'Can I just go out for half an hour to get it?' And Martha, who was really very kind, said that he could.

Of course, they all wanted the day's wish. So Robert hurried to the sand-pit.

The Psammead was waiting for him, but when Robert tried to think of a really good wish, he couldn't, and the others were not there to help him.

Robert couldn't think of a really good wish.

27

'Hurry up,' the Psammead said. 'I can't wait all day.'

'Oh dear,' Robert said. 'I wish that we didn't have to come here to get our wish . . . Oh, don't!'

But it was too late. The Psammead was already making itself big.

'There!' it said. 'That wasn't easy, but I've done it. You don't need to come here to have your wish.'

Robert thanked the Psammead and then hurried back to tell the other children. 'We must wish for something really good tomorrow,' he said.

The next morning they thought and thought, but they couldn't think of a really good wish, so they decided to go to the gravel-pit. Suddenly they saw a baker's boy, who was coming along the road with his basket of bread, and they decided to play a game with him.

'Stop!' cried Cyril.

'Your money or your life!' shouted Robert.

And they stood on each side of the baker's boy.

The baker's boy, who was tall and large, was not very interested and he pushed them both away.

'Don't be stupid!' he said.

But Robert pushed him back and knocked him over. The bread fell out of the boy's basket and went all over the road. The baker's boy was very angry. He hit Robert and they began to fight. But the baker's boy was much bigger and stronger than Robert. He was also not a nice fighter – he pulled Robert's hair, kicked him on the leg, and hit him hard in the stomach. Then he picked up his bread, put it back in the basket, and went on his way.

Cyril wanted to help Robert, but the girls held his arms and stopped him. So Cyril was angry with the girls, and everybody was unhappy. They went along to the gravel-pit, and Robert began to kick the sand angrily.

The bread fell out of the boy's basket.

'I'll teach that baker's boy a lesson one day,' he said. 'I wish I was bigger than him!'

Just then they saw that the Psammead was sitting behind them, and was watching them!

The next minute, Robert had his wish. He was bigger than the baker's boy! Much, much bigger! He was now more than three metres tall! He was not pleased because he looked very strange next to the others, who were still small.

The others felt sorry for him then, and asked the Psammead for another wish. But the Psammead was very cross and unhelpful. 'Why don't you think before you wish?' it said. 'He's a wild, noisy boy, and he can stay like that for the day. It will do him good. Now go away and leave me alone!'

The others turned back to their enormous brother. 'What are we going to do?' they asked.

'First,' said Robert, 'I'm going to get that baker's boy!' And because he had very long legs, he arrived at the bottom of the hill long before the baker's boy, who was stopping at the houses along the road to leave the bread.

Robert hid behind a haystack and waited for the boy. When he saw him coming, he jumped out from behind the haystack and the baker's boy's mouth fell open in surprise. Then Robert took hold of him and put him on top of the haystack.

Robert jumped out from behind the haystack.

'Now get down from there, if you can!' Robert said.

It was very late when the baker's boy got back to the shop, and the baker was very angry!

Then Robert and the others went home, and down to the bottom of the garden. Anthea asked Martha to bring their lunch out there. She knew that Robert was too big to get into the house. Of course, Martha could not see that Robert was much bigger than before, and she only gave him as much meat and potatoes as usual – and no more. Poor Robert was very hungry.

31

Bill stood outside the tent and shouted to the crowd.

The others were feeling unhappy too because there was a fair in town and they wanted to go to it. 'We can't go anywhere now,' Cyril said. 'Not with Robert like this.'

Suddenly Jane cried, 'I know! Let's take Robert to the fair! Someone there will pay us to show him to people. We can make a lot of money.'

The others thought that this was a good plan, and they left at once. When they arrived, they asked to see the head man. His name was Bill, and when he saw Robert, he got very excited.

'How much do you want for him?' he asked.

'You can't *buy* me,' said Robert, 'but I'll come and show myself this afternoon, if you give me fifteen pounds – and some food!'

'Right!' Bill agreed.

So Bill took Robert inside one of the big fair tents and gave him something to eat. But while Robert was eating, Bill put men outside to stop him from escaping.

Then Bill stood outside the tent and began to shout to the crowds. 'Come and see the biggest man in the world!' he cried.

Very soon, people began to stop and listen. A young man and his girlfriend were the first to go and look at Robert. They paid their money to Bill and went in. The people outside heard a loud scream from the girl, and then they all wanted to go in too.

Soon Robert was the most exciting thing to see at the fair, and Bill was making a lot of money. 'Much more than fifteen pounds!' Cyril said to the girls.

Poor Robert got very bored. He had to shake hands with everybody and talk, to show that he was real. And how could he escape at the end of the day? 'They'll kill us when I go small again,' he said.

Cyril thought for a minute. Then he said, 'I've got a plan,' and he went outside the tent to talk to Bill. 'Look here,' he said, 'my brother must be alone when the sun goes down. He gets very strange and angry then. I don't know why, but you must leave him alone, or he'll hurt someone.'

Bill was not very happy about this, but he agreed, and when the sun went down, they left Robert alone. Robert quickly got out under the back wall of the tent, and no one knew who he was because he was just a small boy again.

The children ran all the way home – and we do not know what Bill said when he found that Robert was not there!

Chapter 5

The last wish

The next day there was a letter to say that the children's mother was coming home that afternoon. So they decided to wish for something for their mother. They were busy trying to think of something when Martha came into the room, very excited.

'There were thieves at Lady Chittenden's last night,' she said. 'They took all her jewels! She's got lots of beautiful diamonds – they cost thousands of pounds, I've heard.'

'When I'm older, I'm going to buy Mother jewels like that,' Robert said.

'There were thieves at Lady Chittenden's last night,'
Martha said.

'I'd like Mother to have all Lady Chittenden's beautiful jewels now,' said Jane. 'I wish she could.'

'Oh Jane!' cried the others. 'What have you said?'

'Well, she *will* have them,' said Robert. 'You've wished! Everyone will think she stole them! We'll have to try to find the Psammead and ask it to take the wish back.'

They hurried down to the gravel-pit, but they could not find the Psammead. So they hurried home again and looked in their mother's room for the jewels, but they were not there yet.

'Well, we'll tell Mother about the Psammead, and she'll give back the jewels when they come,' Anthea said.

Cyril shook his head slowly. 'She isn't going to believe us. Can anyone believe about a Psammead if they haven't seen it? And adults never believe things like that. No, she'll think we are the thieves and we'll all go to prison, and everything will be terrible!'

And that afternoon, when Mother came home, the children ran to meet her, and put their arms round her – and tried to stop her from going upstairs to her room.

'But I must take my coat off, and wash my hands!' she cried, laughing. And she went up to her room.

The children went after her – and there, on the table, was a green box. Mother opened it.

'Oh, how beautiful!' she cried.

It was a ring. A beautiful diamond ring.

'Perhaps it's a surprise present from Father,' she said. 'But how did it get here?'

But then she found a diamond necklace – and brooches – and bracelets. There were jewels in every cupboard in her room. The children began to look unhappy, and Jane began to cry.

Mother was no longer smiling. 'Jane, what do you

Then she found a diamond necklace – and brooches – and bracelets.

know about this?' she said slowly. 'The true story, please.'

'We met a sand-fairy, Mother,' Jane began.

'Don't be stupid, Jane,' Mother said angrily.

'Some thieves stole all Lady Chittenden's jewels from her house last night,' Cyril said quickly. 'Perhaps these are *her* jewels!'

Then Mother called for Martha. 'Have any strangers been in this room, Martha?' she asked her.

'Yes, but it was just my young man,' Martha answered, afraid. 'He was moving a heavy cupboard for me.' (This, of course, was Mr Beale, the vicar's nice young servant man, who was now very friendly with Martha.)

So, of course, Mother thought that he was one of the thieves. She would not listen to the children and decided to go at once into town to tell the police. The children could not stop her.

'This is terrible!' said Anthea. 'Poor Martha! And poor Mr Beale – he isn't a thief! What are we going to do?' Then she cried, 'Come on! We must find the Psammead!'

They all hurried down to the gravel-pit, and this time they found the Psammead, sitting on the sand and enjoying the evening sun. When it saw them, it tried to get away, but Anthea put her arms round it. 'Dear, kind Psammead . . .' she began.

Anthea put her arms round the Psammead.

'Oh, you want something, do you?' it said. 'Well, I can't give you any more wishes today.'

'Don't you like giving wishes?' Anthea asked.

'No, I don't,' it said. 'Go away and leave me alone!'

But Anthea went on. 'Listen,' she said. 'If you do what we want today, we'll never ask you for another wish.'

'I'll do anything for that,' it said. 'I really don't enjoy giving wishes. It's very hard work, you know, and I get so tired.'

'Well, first I wish that Lady Chittenden will find that she has never lost her jewels.'

39

The Psammead got bigger, and then went small again. 'Done!' it said.

'I wish that Mother won't get to the police.'

'Done!' the Psammead said again.

'And I wish,' said Jane suddenly, 'that Mother and Martha will forget all about the jewels.'

'Done!' the Psammead said, but its voice was tired. 'Now,' it went on, 'will you wish something for me?'

'Can't you give yourself wishes?' asked Cyril.

'Of course not,' the Psammead said. 'Wish that you will never tell anyone about me.'

'Why?' asked Robert.

'Well, you children always ask for stupid things. But adults aren't like that. If they get hold of me, they'll want to wish for real, important things – like free houses for poor people, and new schools for children everywhere in the country, and money to give to old people. Boring things like that. And they'll find a way to keep them after the sun goes down. And what will happen to the world if all those changes come at once? There'll be terrible trouble. So go on, wish it! Quick!'

Anthea said the Psammead's wish, and it got very, very big. When it was small again, it said, 'Now, I'm very tired. Do you want one last wish?'

'Thank you for everything,' said Jane. 'Have a good long sleep – and I wish that we'll see you again some day.'

Then, for the last time, the Psammead went big, then small again. It looked at them all once more with its long eyes, and then dug itself quickly into the sand.

And when they arrived home again, everything was all right. Mother came home and she and Martha remembered nothing, and Lady Chittenden found that her jewels were not lost.

'Will we ever see the Psammead again, do you think?' Jane said to the others, later in the garden.

And, of course, they did, but not in this story. It was in a very, very different place. It was in a . . . But I must say no more.

Anthea said the Psammead's wish, and it got very, very big.

GLOSSARY

baker a person who makes and sells bread

believe to think that something is real or true

diamond a very expensive, bright stone, often put in rings, etc.

dig (past tense **dug**) to make a hole in the ground

enormous very, very big

fair a kind of travelling market, where you can buy things, play games, watch interesting things, etc.

fairy a person or thing which is not real, but which in stories does wonderful, impossible things

fur the soft hair on an animal's body

Good Heavens! words that show you are very surprised

gravel very small stones

gravel-pit a big hole in the ground or the side of a hill, where people have taken away gravel and sand

jewel a very valuable, expensive stone, e.g. a diamond

kick to hit someone or something with your foot

lemonade a sweet drink made from lemons and sugar

nursemaid a woman servant who helps a mother with her baby

plum a soft, dark-red or purple fruit

Psammead Edith Nesbit's word for a sand-fairy (from a Greek word)

sand very fine, light earth, usually white or yellow (often found on beaches)

servant somebody who works in another person's house

vicar a priest, a man of the church

wish to say what you would like to have or do (usually something which is not possible)

Five Children and It

ACTIVITIES

ACTIVITIES

Before Reading

1 **Read the back cover of the book, and the story introduction on the first page. What do you know now about this story? Tick one box for each sentence.**

	YES	NO
1 The Psammead is thousands of years old.	☐	☐
2 The children found the Psammead in a tree.	☐	☐
3 The Psammead can give three wishes a day.	☐	☐
4 The wishes finish at the end of the day.	☐	☐
5 The Psammead is helpful and friendly.	☐	☐
6 The children always think of really good wishes.	☐	☐

2 **What do the children wish for? Can you guess? Choose some of these wishes and put a tick by them.**

The children wish . . .

- to be very rich.
- to travel back in time.
- to be beautiful.
- to be very, very tall.
- to be different people.

- to be clever.
- to travel forward in time.
- to have adventures.
- to have wings and fly.
- to be very, very small.

Which of these wishes would *you* like to have? Why?

While Reading

Read Chapter 1. Choose the best question-word for these questions, and then answer them.

What / Why

1 . . . did the children do in the gravel-pit?
2 . . . did Anthea scream?
3 . . . was strange about the Psammead's eyes?
4 . . . was Anthea's second wish?
5 . . . did Baby begin to cry loudly?
6 . . . did the children have a terrible afternoon?
7 . . . happened when the sun went down?

Read Chapter 2. Are these sentences true (T) or false (F)? Change the false sentences into true ones.

1 The gold coins were the same as English money.
2 Cyril paid for the lemonade with a gold coin.
3 The children went to Rochester in a horse and cart.
4 Everybody in the shops wanted to take their gold.
5 When they tried to buy a horse and carriage, the man sent for the police.
6 Martha could see the gold coins in Cyril's hands.
7 In the police station the children's pockets were empty.
8 The fairy gold went when the sun came up.

Before you read Chapter 3 (the title is *Wings*), can you guess what happens? Tick one box for each sentence.

	YES	NO
1 The children wish for wings to fly with.	☐	☐
2 They get hungry and have to steal some food.	☐	☐
3 They get into trouble again.	☐	☐
4 They fly home before the sun goes down.	☐	☐

Read Chapter 3, and answer these questions.

1 Why did Jane think it was all right to take the plums?
2 Why did Anthea put some money into the little fat man's pocket?
3 Why didn't people give the children anything to eat?
4 What did the children do on the church roof?
5 Why did the vicar ask about guns?
6 Who took the children home?

Read Chapter 4. Who said these words, and to whom? Who or what were they talking about?

1 'Hurry up. I can't wait all day.'
2 'Don't be stupid!'
3 'He's a wild, noisy boy, and he can stay like that for the day.'
4 'Now get down from there, if you can!'
5 'Someone there will pay us to show him to people.'

6 'Come and see the biggest man in the world!'

7 'They'll kill us when I go small again.'

8 '. . . you must leave him alone, or he'll hurt someone.'

Before you read Chapter 5, can you guess what happens? Choose some of these endings.

The children's next wish is . . .

1 for Martha.   4 something wonderful.

2 for themselves.   5 a terrible mistake.

3 for their mother.   6 their last wish.

Read Chapter 5. Then join these halves of sentences.

1 When Jane heard about Lady Chittenden's jewels, . . .

2 The children wanted to take the wish back, . . .

3 Then their mother came home . . .

4 She thought that Martha's young man was a thief, . . .

5 The children found the Psammead just in time . . .

6 The children's last wish was to see the Psammead again some day, . . .

7 so she went into town to tell the police.

8 but that is another story.

9 she wished that her mother could have the jewels.

10 and found all the stolen jewels in her bedroom.

11 but they couldn't find the Psammead.

12 and their next three wishes stopped all the trouble.

After Reading

1 **Here are the children's wishes in the story. Which happened first? Put them in the right order.**

1 A wish to have beautiful wings to fly with.

2 A wish for their mother to have the stolen jewels.

3 A wish never to tell anyone about the Psammead.

4 A wish for the Psammead to come out of its hole.

5 A wish not to go to the gravel-pit to get their wishes.

6 A wish for Lady Chittenden to find she never lost her jewels.

7 A wish to be very, very beautiful.

8 A wish to see the Psammead again some day.

9 A wish for Martha not to know about the wishes.

10 A wish for their mother not to get to the police.

11 A wish to be very rich.

12 A wish to be bigger than the baker's boy.

13 A wish for their mother and Martha to forget all about the jewels.

2 **Now answer these questions about the children's wishes.**

1 Which wishes got them into trouble?

2 Which wishes got them out of trouble?

3 Which wish did the children enjoy best? (You decide.)

4 Which wish was the best one? (You decide.)

5 Which wish was the worst one? (You decide.)

3 There are fourteen words from the story hidden in this word search. Can you find them?

S	U	W	B	W	O	N	D	E	R	F	U	L	S
T	G	I	E	W	T	E	Y	E	S	H	F	O	T
R	F	N	L	I	C	D	M	Q	E	A	R	S	A
A	U	G	I	S	A	E	C	O	I	N	S	R	L
N	R	S	E	H	F	R	I	E	N	D	L	Y	K
G	R	A	V	E	L	P	I	T	D	S	F	G	S
E	Y	F	E	S	A	N	D	F	A	I	R	Y	N

4 Anthea writes to a friend about the Psammead. Use all the words from the word search to complete her letter.

Last summer we found a _____-_____ in a _____-_____. It was called a Psammead, and it was very _____! It had big _____, and its _____ were on _____. Its body was fat and _____, and it had _____ and feet. It wasn't very _____, but the _____ thing was this – it could give _____! One day we wished for _____ to fly with, and on another day for millions of gold _____. Most people don't _____ in fairies, but our Psammead was real!

    Lots of love, Anthea

Of course, Anthea never sends her letter. Why not?

5 Here is a new illustration for the story. Find the best place in the story to put the picture, and answer these questions.

The picture goes on page ____.

1 Where are the children?
2 What will happen in a few minutes' time?
3 What do the children do when they wake up, and why?

Now write a caption for the illustration.

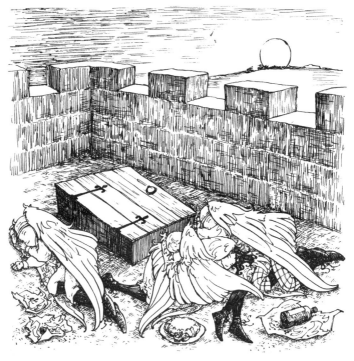

Caption: _____

6 When the children went home, what did the Inspector say to the policeman? Put their conversation in the right order, and write in the speakers' names. The Inspector speaks first (number 3).

1 _____ 'But it's not a crime to buy a horse and carriage.'

2 _____ 'Yes, they did. I saw them. The older boy had pockets full of gold coins. He showed them to me.'

3 _____ 'Why did you bring those four children to the police station?'

4 _____ 'I don't know, sir. I just don't understand it.'

5 _____ 'They didn't steal anything! Gold coins! What gold coins? They didn't have any gold coins!'

6 _____ 'Because they tried to buy a horse and carriage.'

7 _____ 'But his pockets were empty when he was in here. So what did he do with the coins? Eat them?'

8 _____ 'No, but they tried to pay with these strange gold coins. I think they stole them.'

7 What was the Psammead thinking at the end of the story? Complete this passage. Use as many words as you like.

'Good. They've gone. Now I _____ a very deep hole and have a _____. Why do children always wish for _____, like gold coins and wings? Of course, adults are no better. They _____ real, important things, like _____. That makes terrible trouble, so I hope nobody finds me again for _____.'

ABOUT THE AUTHOR

Edith Nesbit was born in London in 1858, but spent many of her early years in France and Germany. She did not like school – she tried to run away from one of them – but she loved reading, and read every book that she could find. The family returned to England, and in 1880 Edith married Hubert Bland. When Hubert became ill, and a business friend ran away with all his money, Edith had to work to make money for them both, so she wrote poems and stories for newspapers.

She went on writing all her life, which was a very busy one. She had five children (two of them were adopted), and she was a very 'modern' woman for the times. She cut her hair short, wore woollen clothes, and helped to start the Fabian Society (a political group). In 1899 she and Hubert moved to Kent, to a beautiful old house called Well Hall, which Edith loved. There, the Blands became famous for their weekend house-parties, which included many well-known writers. Hubert died in 1914, and Edith's life became very unhappy for a while, but later she married again. She died in Kent in 1924.

Edith Nesbit herself said she was 'a child in a grown-up world', and in her writing she never forgot what it was like to be a child. Her famous books for children include *The Story of the Treasure Seekers* (1899) and *The Railway Children* (1906), a much-loved story which has been filmed many times. *Five Children and It* (1902) was filmed for television in 1992, and children still enjoy the magic and excitement of the story. Magic wishes in everyday life make all kinds of trouble, and as the Psammead said, 'Why don't you *think* before you wish?'

ABOUT BOOKWORMS

OXFORD BOOKWORMS LIBRARY
Classics • True Stories • Fantasy & Horror • Human Interest
Crime & Mystery • Thriller & Adventure

The OXFORD BOOKWORMS LIBRARY offers a wide range of original and adapted stories, both classic and modern, which take learners from elementary to advanced level through six carefully graded language stages:

Stage 1 (400 headwords)	**Stage 4** (1400 headwords)
Stage 2 (700 headwords)	**Stage 5** (1800 headwords)
Stage 3 (1000 headwords)	**Stage 6** (2500 headwords)

More than fifty titles are also available on cassette, and there are many titles at Stages 1 to 4 which are specially recommended for younger learners. In addition to the introductions and activities in each Bookworm, resource material includes photocopiable test worksheets and Teacher's Handbooks, which contain advice on running a class library and using cassettes, and the answers for the activities in the books.

Several other series are linked to the OXFORD BOOKWORMS LIBRARY. They range from highly illustrated readers for young learners, to playscripts, non-fiction readers, and unsimplified texts for advanced learners.

Oxford Bookworms Starters   *Oxford Bookworms Factfiles*
Oxford Bookworms Playscripts   *Oxford Bookworms Collection*

Details of these series and a full list of all titles in the OXFORD BOOKWORMS LIBRARY can be found in the *Oxford English* catalogues. A selection of titles from the OXFORD BOOKWORMS LIBRARY can be found on the next pages.

Alice's Adventures in Wonderland

LEWIS CARROLL

Retold by Jennifer Bassett

There, on top of the mushroom, was a large caterpillar, smoking a pipe. After a while the Caterpillar took the pipe out of its mouth and said to Alice in a slow, sleepy voice, 'Who are *you*?'

What strange things happen when Alice falls down the rabbit-hole and into Wonderland! She has conversations with the Caterpillar and the Cheshire Cat, goes to the Mad Hatter's tea party, plays croquet with the King and Queen of Hearts . . .

The Jungle Book

RUDYARD KIPLING

Retold by Ralph Mowat

In the jungle of Southern India the Seeonee Wolf-Pack has a new cub. He is not a wolf – he is Mowgli, a human child, but he knows nothing of the world of men. He lives and hunts with his brothers the wolves. Baloo the bear and Bagheera the panther are his friends and teachers. And Shere Khan, the man-eating tiger, is his enemy.

Kipling's famous story of Mowgli's adventures in the jungle has been loved by young and old for more than a hundred years.

Anne of Green Gables

L. M. MONTGOMERY

Retold by Clare West

Marilla Cuthbert and her brother Matthew want to adopt an orphan, to help on the farm at Green Gables. They ask for a boy, but they get Anne, who has red hair and freckles, and who talks and talks and talks.

They didn't want a girl, but how can they send a child back, like an unwanted parcel? So Anne stays, and begins a new life in the sleepy, quiet village of Avonlea in Canada.

But it is not so quiet after Anne comes to live there . . .

Matty Doolin

CATHERINE COOKSON

Retold by Diane Mowat

Matty is fifteen and is leaving school in a few weeks' time. He wants to work with animals, and would like to get a job on a farm. But his parents say he's too young to leave home – he must stay in the town and get a job in ship-building, like his father. They also say he can't go on a camping holiday with his friends. And they say he can't keep his dog, Nelson, because Nelson barks all day and eats his father's shoes.

But it is because of Nelson that Matty finds a new life . . .

BOOKWORMS • HUMAN INTEREST • STAGE 2

Too Old to Rock and Roll and Other Stories

JAN MARK

Retold by Diane Mowat

Greg is a teenager with a problem – his father. After the death of Greg's mother in an accident, his father takes no interest in life at all. Greg tries hard to help him. His father is too old to rock and roll, of course . . . or is he?

These short stories by Jan Mark look at life, love, and friendship through teenagers' eyes.

BOOKWORMS • HUMAN INTEREST • STAGE 3

The Railway Children

EDITH NESBIT

Retold by John Escott

'We have to leave our house in London,' Mother said to the children. 'We're going to live in the country, in a little house near a railway line.'

And so begins a new life for Roberta, Peter, and Phyllis. They become the railway children – they know all the trains, Perks the station porter is their best friend, and they have many adventures on the railway line.

But why has their father had to go away? Where is he, and will he ever come back?

R53271